SERVICE WITH A SMILE

SERVICE WITH A SMILE

✦

A Practical Guide for Waiters and Waitresses

Esther Karvelas

iUniverse, Inc.

New York Lincoln Shanghai

SERVICE WITH A SMILE
A Practical Guide for Waiters and Waitresses

iUniverse books may be ordered through booksellers or by contacting:

iUniverse
2021 Pine Lake Road, Suite 100
Lincoln, NE 68512
www.iuniverse.com
1-800-Authors (1-800-288-4677)

ISBN-13: 978-0-595-35736-9 (pbk)
ISBN-13: 978-0-595-80213-5 (ebk)
ISBN-10: 0-595-35736-9 (pbk)
ISBN-10: 0-595-80213-3 (ebk)

Printed in the United States of America

I dedicate this book to all hard-working waiters and waitresses—they are the foundation of any successful restaurant business.

Special thanks to my cousin Cathy Protos for her valuable assistance in making this book a reality.

Contents

Introduction

The goal of this book is to help you succeed as a food server. It is not an easy job, but it is not as difficult as many make it seem. Most problems arise due to a lack of training. Sometimes a person will take years to learn what others have learned in a much shorter period. Others will be quick learners, will be naturals at service, or will be lucky to have started out in a restaurant that had outstanding training procedures. If you do not fit into any of these categories, where do you turn? This is a problem, because there is no resource such professionals can rely on—until now.

Food service is an occupation you can be proud of. It is a talent that you can learn. The experience can be interesting, educational, and rewarding. You have the option to work full time or part time. There is so much latitude, and such a variety of places to work, that almost anyone can find a job to suit her needs—provided, of course, that she is willing to learn the trade and improve her skills. I intend to teach you a variety of skills to help you achieve your potential and obtain your goals.

What This Book Won't Talk About

This book will not cover other jobs in the food-service industry. It is not going to discuss the advantages and disadvantages of various restaurant types. It will not discuss the variety of foods that restaurants serve, nor will it discuss the pros and cons of the various techniques of restaurant management. Areas such as menus, advertising, promotions, contests, and so forth are the responsibility of the owners or managers as they attempt to increase sales. The food server will often see the positive and negative aspects of these sales tools, and this book will discuss how the server can take advantage of them, but it will not evaluate their merits.

1

Job Opportunities

Serving is probably one of the easiest jobs one can get. It offers immediate monetary rewards through tips, and the work hours are very flexible. In addition to providing a regular paycheck, a food-service job also often provides you with a discount on food, or even free food. This type of job also gives you the opportunity to pursue other goals in life, such as furthering your education or increasing your income in retirement.

It is a hard job, you will have many helping hands: the cook, the bus boys, the dishwashers, management, etc. The server only needs to concentrate on the customers. You can make food service a career or use it as a stepping-stone to getting what you want in life. Not bad!

Advantages

The restaurant industry offers flexible work hours that most other businesses cannot offer. Shifts in dinner houses may require a server to work two to four hours, while a twenty-four-hour restaurant will offer graveyard shifts. Students, moonlighters, mothers with baby-sitting concerns, and even full-time employees can normally find some restaurant whose schedule accommodates their other commitments. A part-time server can often make more money than a full-time worker can at another type of job.

2

How to Fill Out an Application: Dos and Don'ts

Most restaurant applications are easy to complete. However, do not include more information than necessary. For example, if you are applying for a server position but you used to own your own business or manage another restaurant, do not volunteer that information. It will not help you get the job as a server, because you may be considered overqualified or unqualified. And *always* leave the salary section negotiable.

Your Own Business

No owner wants to know your history. They are more interested in what you are willing to do for *their* establishment. Do not talk about your life experiences, past successes, or failures unless they ask you about them. This information will not help you get the position, and excessive boasting or attempts to impress the boss with your knowledge may end up costing you the job.

3

Preparing for Your New Job

Training

Most restaurants will train you on the spot by having you job-shadow, or follow another experienced server, for two or three days. This training will give you, the new server, time to get acquainted with the restaurant procedures and routine as well as time to get to know where everything is. It will also provide you with the necessary support that is so important to anyone starting a new job.

With the advent of modern technology, most restaurants have done away with the old-fashioned meal tickets, checkbooks, menus, and customers' checks and have adopted a computerized system. You must become familiar with this technology. This may take a few hours or a few days. The trick to becoming a successful server is to ask many questions and to be patient, confident, and determined. Resist becoming discouraged if you find the job challenging at first. Your persistence will pay off.

Menus

There are many things to learn when you go to work for a new restaurant, even if you are an experienced server. Don't be afraid to ask questions or take notes. Take a menu home and study it. Knowing the menu should be your top priority. You should memorize prices, specials of the day, soups, desserts, and other special menus, such as those offered for children.

If a customer asks a specific question about an item on the menu or in the meal, you should know which section of the menu you can refer them to. Know where on the menu to find appetizers, entrées, and desserts. This will not only help you avoid the embarrassment of causing delays in the order, but it will inspire confidence in your customers and bosses, and you will benefit from increased self-confidence. You cannot be a professional at your job if you don't know what you are selling. Therefore, study the menu and the products on it.

Where Everything Is

In order to carry out your responsibilities, you must know where to find everything you will need. Take a tour of the restaurant. Learn what is in each reach-in, walk-in, freezer, and dry-storage area. Occasions will arise—usually when it's busy—when your customer needs something and no one is around to help you find it. If you rely on someone else to tell you where things are, you may come to suffer for it—in your pocketbook.

Promotions and Discounts

Some restaurants offer customer promotions or discounts in the form of complimentary dinners, free desserts, coupons, two-for-ones, and so on. Learn the restaurant's policy regarding these promotions and discounts. One very popular discount is the one for senior citizens. Some restaurants are firm about the limitations of the discounts, such as who should receive them and when they are in effect. Most are not. Be careful not to offend the customer by taking it upon yourself to decide who should or should not get the discount, especially if you are new. Many customers will be regulars who know more about the restaurant's policies than a new employee. Unless the restaurant you work for demands it, don't make a big deal about proof of age or time restrictions, as you do not want to lose repeat business. In short, be aware of promotional offers and honor them.

Meals

Most restaurants have some kind of employee meal policy. They may provide special meals for employees only or provide a discount. Often, this policy is regulated by state law. Whatever the policy, it usually offers employees a reasonably good deal. Don't be the employee who decides that you won't honor the meal policy and instead help yourself to ice cream, pies, soup, and mistakes by cooks when no one is looking. In many cases, you will jeopardize your job. Consider the employee meal policy a benefit. Compare the price of your employee meal to what it would cost you to buy a similar item at another restaurant, or to prepare the meal at home, and the savings may impress you.

Policy Lost in the Details

Adhere to company policies. Management cannot allow the employees to do whatever they want. Sounds obvious, doesn't it? However, some managers tend to play "Mr. Nice Guy," to be lax about the requirements, or to be otherwise unobservant of situations in which employees disregard policies. Before long, no one knows why sales are down. Not paying attention to details will eventually, and inevitably, lead to lost customers.

For example, say a server forgets part of the uniform, is wearing shoes that have not been approved, or has a new and wild hairstyle that does not meet with the restaurant's policy. Or, imagine that servers are more interested in talking to one another than to attending to their customers, or that a cook decides to change the plate setup. These are but a few of the things that can go unobserved and unresolved over a period of weeks or months.

These small and seemingly unimportant details can create a monstrous problem that can take years to correct. When management seems to be getting tough on policy, understand that, although their concerns may seem petty, the change may be good for both yourself and the establishment in the end.

4

Appearances

As a server, you are in the public eye, and customers will likely scrutinize you from head to toe. Remember that you represent the restaurant for which you work. Your personal appearance and hygiene will always be open to criticism. Therefore, in addition to using common sense, follow the policies and guidelines below.

Aprons

Many restaurants require the server to wear a uniform, usually including an apron. Remember that the apron is often at a seated customer's eye level. The customer can't help but notice it, particularly if it is wrinkled or dirty. You should always make sure that your apron is clean and pressed. Even if it is in perfect condition when you get to work, if you aren't careful, it won't take long before it starts looking like you have been wearing it for a week. Whatever you do, don't use it to dry your hands. It is a good idea to keep a clean and ironed spare apron in your locker at work for emergencies.

Fingernails

Your hands are constantly in front of the customers, and they will notice your fingernails, especially if they are untrimmed, dirty, or poorly maintained. Many restaurants have policies regarding long nails and nail polish—especially concerning wild colors. Extra long nails may be attractive, but they are not practical for a server. Subtle nail polish shades and shorter nails will be easier to maintain and more pleasing to the majority of customers.

Hair

Some restaurants prefer that a server wear either short hair or hair that can be pulled back tightly off the face. Many establishments still require hairnets. However, others will be lenient toward your hairstyle. Some styles may appear sloppy and unclean by their nature, even if they are not. Obviously, many customers will find this distasteful. There is nothing appetizing about long hair almost touching the food that you are serving. If you want long hair, spend time securing it properly before going to work. If you fail to do this, your hairstyle will probably start coming loose halfway through your shift. If the restaurant is busy, you probably won't have time to do a repair job, and you may appear careless and unkempt.

Shoes

Since you will spend most of your working hours on your feet, high-quality shoes are very important. When you purchase

your shoes, make sure they meet your employer's requirements and are comfortable. Many restaurants allow different
styles and colors, avoid the temptation to buy shoes that you
can wear for both work and leisure. The shoes you purchase
should be for work purposes only, and always make sure they
are polished and clean. It may also be a good idea to find shoes
with non-skid soles. High heels are tiring and can be danger-
ous. It is best to avoid them, unless they are required in your
work area.

Jewelry

Compared to policies of the past, today there is greater latitude toward wearing a variety of jewelry. If you are allowed to
wear jewelry at your workplace, don't be excessive. If a chain
or bracelet interferes with your work, especially if it is loose fitting, leave it at home. Make sure you know what the dress
code allows—many restaurants limit what you can wear
because of safety rules.

Jewelry gives you an opportunity to enhance your appearance and improve your overall presentation to the customer. It
can help you look professional, but not if you overdo it. You
may want to choose jewelry specifically for work, such as a few
pieces that go well with your uniform. If you need help, ask
people whose judgment you respect for their opinions.

Sweaters

You should always be aware of your overall appearance in the workplace. Sometimes you may need to wear a sweater in the restaurant. Make sure it is clean and, as much as possible, coordinated with your uniform. A torn, dirty, or poorly fitting sweater will likely catch the customer's attention and detract from the positive aspects of your appearance. A neat, tasteful sweater should always blend in with the rest of the uniform so that the customer hardly notices anything out of the ordinary.

Pockets

Occasionally, you will meet a server who carries all kinds of things in his pockets—an individual creamer or even an entire bottle of ketchup. This may appear to make sense, since he can retrieve the item quickly and efficiently. But it's a big mistake: besides what it does to the server's appearance, it is tasteless to pull something out of your pocket and set it on the customer's table. If you don't have room on your tray or in your hands, make another trip. You should never carry anything in your pocket except perhaps money, a checkbook, a corkscrew, or a pen. Picture the atmosphere in a high-class restaurant, and then imagine a server walking around in that restaurant with a bottle of ketchup in his pocket. It sounds absurd, yet it happens all the time—with tea bags, sweeteners, and even silverware.

Others' Appearance

It is also your responsibility as a server to observe whether your coworkers are neatly groomed and attired. If you see that a server or bus person is looking sloppy or dirty (for example, wearing a wrinkled shirt, a dirty vest or apron, uncombed hair, or an unshaven beard), bring it to the management's attention. These things all reflect on the quality of the restaurant. Whether you realize it or not, another employee's appearance can affect how the customer sees you and your service. By contrast, sharp and neatly dressed servers and bus people tell the customer that this is a better-than-average establishment, and they will conduct themselves accordingly, even in tipping. You may not feel comfortable saying something directly to the person about his appearance, but you can make the management aware of the situation.

Cell Phones

Servers and cell phones are a bad combination in the workplace. Many employees disregard restaurant policies restricting the use of cell phones. These employees hide in the washrooms or in remote areas to use their phones. Avoid doing this at all costs, such a bad habit makes it easier to ignore or forget your customers.

5

Stations

Rotating Stations

Management may insist on rotating stations for fairness and cross-training of employees. It will help you if you know how to work at different stations. You should push for the experience to learn the different areas of responsibility as much as possible. It will make you a much more valuable employee and give you greater flexibility in the hours and shifts you can choose. You will also have the opportunity to meet many more customers as regulars have a tendency to want to sit in the same place.

Staying Close By

Once you have been assigned a station, stay near it as much as possible. Pay attention to your customers to observe and anticipate opportunities to give them better service. There is a tendency to get sidetracked in the back of the restaurant, especially during slow periods. Look for things to do to keep busy out on the floor. Customers find it extremely annoying to have to seek out their server, especially if they have to leave their table to find service. Don't let this happen to your customers.

Focus

Your primary focus should be on your station and the number of tables and customers in your station. It should not matter to you if the restaurant is busy or if there is a line of people waiting outside. Remember that you are only responsible for taking care of your section. Leave the rest up to the owner, manager, or other coworkers, unless you are asked to help.

It is up to you to keep your mind and your eyes on your station. Most customers will only slightly wave when they are trying to get your attention. Very seldom will someone raise his voice, tap a glass, or in some way draw too much attention while trying to get yours. The average customer will let things slide and will not be pleased about you being unobservant. Of course, this would give that customer a good reason to reduce your tip.

You will be saving time and increasing your customers' satisfaction if you constantly try to anticipate their requests. As you serve the drinks, main course, and dessert, always make sure that you check with the customers and for yourself that everything is all right before leaving their table. Avoid looking rushed. If you are not calm or if you lack control of the situation, your customer will feel ill at ease. Oftentimes, customers sense when they are keeping you, especially if your voice and actions express impatience. They will usually help you out by saying everything is just fine, when it really isn't. After you leave the table, they may remember something they want. This creates a problem for you and for them. They keep thinking about this thing they want, and when they are able to flag you down, you have to say you'll be with them in a moment or stop what you are doing to help them. Avoid this problem by doing things right the first time. Remember that you are selling the whole dining experience: a beginning, a middle, and an end.

Don't Step on It

Everything about your station's appearance, even the floor surrounding your area, is going to affect how the customer feels about the restaurant and your service. You may say that is obviously not your responsibility, but do you want the customer's first impression to be poor because the floor around their table is covered with crackers, breadcrumbs, or other assorted foods? If you can't find a bus person to do the job, grab the broom and dustpan or the carpet sweeper and clean the area before the customer is seated. Remember, it is your customer and your tip!

Cutlery

Always be tactful when it comes to replacing soiled cutlery. Simply remove the article and replace it with a clean one without giving a reason or excuse. Customers do not want to hear that the dishwasher is too busy or behind in her work or that the restaurant has run out of clean cutlery. It is always the server's responsibility to make sure that the customer has the necessary place setting and that everything is clean.

Towels

Clean towels are an absolute necessity. If you are wiping tables with a dirty towel, the end result will be a smeared and smelly table. An over-bleached towel also leaves an unappetizing odor. You must be aware of what products the bus person is using. Customers at adjoining tables may be watching as a table is being cleaned, so don't fool yourself into thinking that no one will notice a dirty towel. Be careful that an overly wet towel doesn't leave the table that way, and make sure that the table is dry before putting out new place settings.

Take Your Time

Each table you wait on must seem as though it is the only one in your station. No matter how busy you are, try to avoid giving your customers the impression that you are pressed for time. In many cases, this will only put them ill at ease and make them nervous. They will try to hurry their order, and this will usually cause problems. You are better off to tell them that they can take their time and that you will check back with them in a few minutes.

In many instances, customers will ask for your assistance in making their selection. Many of your customers will be indecisive. Don't let that upset you. You are considered an expert, and many customers will ask for your advice, particularly if it is their first time at that particular restaurant. If you help your customers choose, it will make it more comfortable for them and faster for you. Obviously, the better you know the menu and any specials for the day, the better equipped you are to make everything run smoothly.

End of Shift

All restaurants should have procedures for closing down a station or turning it over to another server. It may be the restaurant's policy to stop waiting on new customers anywhere from fifteen to thirty minutes prior to changing shifts. Never leave without making sure you have completely finished your side work. Think about the person who will be following you into the station you are leaving. If your customers are not finished with their meals and you are going to turn them over to someone else, continue to assure them good service by informing the next server of exactly what still needs to be done. For instance, the customers may want dessert or after dinner drinks. Always make sure the customers' checks are given to the next server. Remember, the customers may still be at the restaurant after you leave. You are on the clock—they are not.

Be Flexible

Occasions may arise when you are asked to stay beyond your scheduled shift. More often than not, management will expect you to be ready to clock out at your scheduled time. However, when conditions dictate, the customer must come first. Working in the restaurant business is not always a predictable job, and more often than not, scheduling will be a give-and-take experience for both management and employees alike. There will be times when you may want a special shift or day off, so be willing to reciprocate.

6

Having More Than One Relationship

One Big Happy Family

When you work with fellow employees long enough, some of them may become very good friends. They can even become like family.

In the meantime, because there are so many different personalities and temperaments, it takes some effort to get along with everyone. Remember that the others are making an effort to get along with you as well. Especially when you are a new employee, other employees will size you up. Restaurants are a people business, whether the people are fellow employees or customers. Learn the subtleties of workplace friendships, and they will carry right into your relationships with the customers. And, guess who benefits the most?

Owners and Servers

In the workplace, the relationship between the owner and the server should be of a professional nature. That is not to say that you should avoid becoming friends, just that the friendship should not interfere with the server's job. A server should also try to keep his friendships at a professional distance, since his position may be jeopardized or compromised in the event of a personal misunderstanding or problem in the workplace. The same also holds true for the owner, whose integrity could be undermined by a jealous server. Secret or delicate information could be exposed to the public, hurting the business as well as the server's future job prospects.

Teamwork

All employees are responsible for establishing teamwork by helping their fellow workers. If someone looks as if she needs help, see if you can do something for her, by helping to clean her station, for example. If everyone is concerned about fellow employees, everyone's job becomes easier and more pleasant.

Often restaurant employees will trade shifts or work longer hours than they are supposed to, covering for someone who wants to leave early. Restaurant employees seem more willing to help each other than employees in other businesses. Possibly because of the pressure caused by frequently hectic meal periods, they band together to accomplish their objectives. When employees work together, sales typically reflect their cooperation. If employees do not cooperate, profits will decline and everyone will suffer instead of prospering.

Respecting Management

Some employees show little, if any, respect for manage-ment—this may be rightly so, because some managers deserve no respect. However, whether the management deserves respect or not, they are still in charge and can either help you or give you problems. Managers are not supposed to have favorites, but it is realistic to expect that most will. Getting along with even the most disagreeable ones will benefit you. Better hours, time off, and good stations are but a few exam-ples of the value of a good relationship with management. Managers will either improve your opportunity to make more money, or they will not—how they treat you depends largely on how you treat them.

In summary, respect those who have the positions of authority. Whether they are young or old, qualified or not, deserving or undeserving, they are still in charge. Moreover, try to understand management's role. They often work long hours, usually under very stressful conditions. Give them rein-forcement, and it will normally pay you dividends.

Dishwashers

Situations can arise where a dishwasher can be of great help to you as a server. Occasionally, reward him with a couple of dol-lars, or cigarettes if he is a smoker. It won't be forgotten. Likely, you will be the only person that does anything extra for him. The more people in the restaurant that are willing to help you, the better quality service you will be able to provide your customers. Remember, you can save a few dollars in the short term by not being concerned about your coworkers, or you can have many people helping you reach your maximum by keeping them all in mind. Think smart, and think big!

Cooks

A smart server realizes that the better the relationship is between her and the cooks, the more cooperative the cooks will be with her. Cooking can be a tough job, and many cooks can be difficult to work with, often becoming extremely temperamental. The kitchen is normally very hot, and cooks spend much of their time working under high pressure. Your words of understanding and encouragement will go a long way toward building a good rapport. You may even want to consider giving the cook an occasional small gift. Remember birthdays, special occasions, and particularly difficult or busy shifts with cards, cigarettes, or money. Those same cooks will reciprocate by helping you—the plates will look better and the food will be hotter.

Bus People

Most restaurants employ bus people. They too can be very valuable to you. If you take care of them, they will take care of you. They help to stock the stations, clean and set the tables, fill water glasses, and pour coffee, along with other duties. Treat them with respect, and don't forget to tip them. They will make money for you by providing your customers with good service. As with the cooks, the better you work with them as a team, the more professional you will appear.

Food Expeditors

Some restaurants employ "food expeditors." This person's only responsible is to bring food from the kitchen to the table. You, the server, must always be conscious of your customers' needs. Always return to your table to see if your customers have the right order or to see if they would like something else. Show them that you are still their server.

7

You and Your Relationships: Your Overall Conduct

In addition to your physical appearance, you must also consider other factors in your overall conduct: your willingness to get along and support your coworkers and your responsibility to look after your customers. I cannot overstate the importance of maintaining positive interaction with customers: your personality, tone of voice, facial expressions, level of composure in stressful situations, and rapport you have established in the workplace will all contribute to your success as a server. In order to be convincing and seem natural, you must constantly be aware of these qualities and try to maintain them during your working hours with everyone you encounter.

You and the Boss (Who Are You Kidding?)

There are individuals in every business who contribute by bearing more than their share of the workload, while others rarely complete their own work satisfactorily, much less do anything extra (except when they think the boss might be watching them; then they want to appear like a busy worker bee). Management will figure out what is going on sooner rather than later. The quality of your work will give you just rewards, either positive or negative. It's up to you.

You and the Cook (Small Details Can Make Big Profits)

Don't be afraid to question the quality of an item when it comes up in the call window. If it is obvious that a steak is not properly cooked, or if you receive a plate with food that looks almost inedible, say something to the cook or management. Know what the procedure is for returning food, and try to be tactful. New cooks or extremely busy shifts are not valid excuses for poor quality. Don't make the customer suffer. If you do, you and the restaurant will lose in the end. Again, be polite when relating the problem to the cook, and avoid causing a big scene.

You and the Customer (You Never Know)

Often, a server will pay more attention to a table ordering high-priced items. A server may give better service or devote extra time to these customers and forget the tables ordering less expensive meals. Customers may order less expensive items for many reasons. One reason may be that they eat out more often, another reason may be health concerns, or it may come down to plain economics. Someone who orders a less expensive item is not necessarily a poor tipper. Be careful not to make rash judgments as to who is going to leave a good tip. Looks and first impressions can be deceiving.

You and the Workplace (Can You Hear Yourself Think?)

Be aware of how the restaurant environment sounds to the customers. Noise levels in many restaurants can be controlled. Employees of even the best restaurants often make such a racket that they begin to sound like a greasy spoon diner. Imagine the sound of dishes being carelessly thrown in bus trays, servers talking (and sometimes yelling) to cooks, hostesses and cashiers talking about seating, and so on. All of this can get out of hand and disrupt an otherwise excellent dining experience. Especially during busy periods, twenty to thirty employees can make an incredible amount of noise. Consider how loud the environment is and how it may affect your tip. Handle yourself with a touch of class, and if you notice poor noise control where you work, tactfully suggest to the management that they look into rectifying the problem.

Large Groups

Especially for an inexperienced server, a large order can be a very trying experience. Stay calm and stay organized. Normally, problems arise when the person handling the order gets upset. You may start out with confidence, but then something goes wrong, and before you know it, a disaster is in the making.

The key to handling large parties is proper training and a thorough knowledge of the restaurant's procedures. If you have this knowledge, you will be confident that you are in total control of the situation. Avoid making mistakes in the beginning especially, as it will be difficult to recover and take the rest of the order correctly. By using a firm yet polite approach, you will show the customers that you know what you are doing. Before the order goes into the kitchen, make sure you are aware of any drinks, salads, or soups needed and that you know to whom they should go. Many restaurants will have you make notes to yourself. The best approach is to have everything out on the table before the entrées come. Then all you need to do is deliver the entrées and take care of any last-minute requests. Make sure you know who ordered first, and deliver the food to the table in the same direction as the one you went in when taking the order. Also, verify that the order is complete. If something is missing, you want the cook to be aware of it as soon as possible.

During the meal, keep the table as clear of dishes and glasses as possible. An uncluttered table is visually appealing and will help you stay organized. If you have other customers, avoid spending long periods with the large party. You are better off checking with the large party frequently than getting bogged down with them. If you give good service to a large party but your other customers suffer, you too will suffer monetarily. Don't get sidetracked, especially if the large party tends to demand too much of your attention. If you see that the party is going to be a problem, ask for help from management, other servers, and especially bus people. Bus people can be of great assistance in handling large parties by providing additional set-ups, water, and coffee and by keeping the table cleared. Ask for their help, and don't be afraid to reward them, especially if the restaurant doesn't have a tip-sharing policy.

Large groups can be time-consuming, demanding, sometimes boisterous, and sometimes inattentive to the server. Remember, though, that they can also be very profitable. Remain calm and in control, take your time, get it right from the start, and show them that you are the consummate professional.

Separate Checks

It is incumbent upon the server to ask if the customers would like one check or separate checks. This will prevent problems at the end for both the server and the customers. Remember that you, the server, are obligated to ask. A bit of foresight here will go a long way.

Carry Your Own Load

It is perfectly acceptable to ask for help if you are exceptionally busy. However, you should be careful not to do this too often. The habit of asking the manager, the owner, or the other employees to do your work can get old very quickly. If it becomes obvious, others will think you are not able to handle your job. Each person is hired to take care of a certain part of the workload. Give it your best effort, and you usually won't have a problem. Otherwise, you might soon be looking for employment elsewhere.

8

You and the Customer

Meeting a Variety of People

Restaurants are places where you will meet an exciting variety of people: people with different social, cultural, and educational backgrounds. Talking to the customers can be a learning experience for you. It also shows customers that you are interested in them and care about them as individuals. Be careful, though, that you don't get involved in long, drawn-out conversations. Have a couple of ideas on how to get away from those who might keep you from tending to your other customers. Remember to do this in a polite manner to avoid offending the customer.

How to Welcome the Customer

Always approach your customers with a friendly smile. You might want to greet your customers with a kind expression of welcome, especially if they are regular customers or if it is a family restaurant. Use phrases such as "How was your weekend?" "It's nice to see you again," or "I hope you had a nice vacation." This is not to say that you should chat for long periods. Keep your contact on a professional basis. If you know your customers by name, welcome them by name—customers usually like that. If they are steady customers whose names you do not know, greet them in the same friendly manner.

Customers Who Change Tables

Deal tactfully with customers who wish to change tables. As their server, you should explain the difficulty that table switching would cause if the table they wish to change to does not belong to your section. This may cause confusion, especially if an order has already been placed. Of course, you are not justified in showing disapproval or getting angry. You must still offer the best service possible to avoid offending the customers—even if resulting problems are their fault.

Customers Who Share Meals

Some customers like to share meals, and there is usually a good reason for this, especially if they are seniors. Sometimes they have health concerns, or perhaps the reasons are economic. Some restaurants serve portions that may be too big for one person. Whatever the reason, the server should always handle meal sharing in a professional and courteous manner. Never look down on customers for their choice.

Not Being Efficient Enough

No one wants to drink out of a chipped, cracked, or lipstick-stained glass or cup, and yet most people have experienced this at some time while dining. There are various reasons why these instances occur. Perhaps the dishwasher or bus person is very busy, there is a problem with the dishwasher, or the kitchen is understaffed. All of these reasons are insufficient. There are plenty of steps you can take to prevent a stained or chipped glass from reaching a customer's table.

Even though ensuring clean place settings may take effort from the dishwasher and the bus person, it is ultimately the server's responsibility. The server should always make a point of checking the place settings in their section to make sure that everything is as it should be.

Being Too Efficient

As a server, you will be relied on to use good judgment and common sense. One area that typically causes difficulty for a new server is knowing when to place the customer's meal ticket into the kitchen. Get to know how long different items take to come out of the kitchen—this will depend on the time of the day, how many cooks are in the kitchen, which particular cooks are present, and whether the restaurant is busy. All of these factors will affect the cooking time. For instance, if the customers are having cocktails, appetizers, and salads, make sure that you don't put the rest of the order into the kitchen right away if they are only going to take a few minutes to show up in the window. Remember that the customer, especially at dinnertime, will not be in a hurry. It is very annoying to receive an entrée when you were not expecting it for another five or ten minutes. Most customers will let you know if they are in a hurry. Usually, they have come to eat and relax. They have come to your restaurant to sit down and be waited on in a friendly and warm atmosphere. Don't make them feel as though your restaurant is competing with fast food places. Make sure they realize that you have offered them an alternative. You are their efficient server, but don't be too efficient. Read the customer's mood. Tune yourself into each table, and try to serve your customers accordingly.

Treating Customers Equally

You should always give the same kind of service to all your customers regardless of how many tables you may have or how busy your station might be. You should never spend too much time with one table at the expense of other customers. Dividing your time equally will not only help you avoid complaints, but it will ensure none of your customers feel ignored.

Things Not to Discuss with Customers

a. Politics

b. Religion

c. Sex

It is difficult to know what your customer's beliefs are or what they would like to hear. Sometimes you may not even be sure of your own position on a certain topic. It is not important. What is important is to smile, be charming, and avoid discussing these topics. These are delicate subjects that never can be resolved in a matter of a few minutes. Simply dismiss yourself from the table politely. Engaging in such topics may cause you to lose the current customer, future customers, or even your job.

Don't Gossip

Gossip usually undermines the integrity of a server. Whether the discussion is about your boss, manager, other servers, the restaurant, the food, or whatever else, gossiping will invariably cause friction in the workplace. The gossip you start may even be spread to other employees by the customers themselves.

Customers' Tables (Don't Step on It)

Customers' tables should always be clean and free of any dirt or grease. All condiment containers should be full and replenished as necessary. Booths should be kept clean of breadcrumbs and other debris.

If the restaurant uses tablecloths, make sure to check them carefully and replace them if any soil is present. Chairs should be clean and should always match the seating arrangements. You should do your part to replace missing articles or chairs at the station and not wait for the bus person or management to do it.

High Chairs or Booster Chairs

It is especially important to keep high chairs and booster chairs very clean. These articles usually require more care than regular seats. You should always offer a high chair or booster chair to a family with children before they ask you to bring one to the table. This will impress the customers by showing them that you are anticipating their every need. Always compliment the customers' children as a way of welcoming them to the restaurant and providing a positive atmosphere.

Most restaurants have children's menus, coloring books, toys, and so on. Again, always offer these items to the family, and do not wait to be asked. Let your customers see that you are a caring and observant server, ready to handle all of their needs and working to make them as comfortable as possible.

Time Wise

A server should always look to decrease the amount of time she needs to serve her customers properly. For example, if you have four or five tables and two have asked for coffee, it would be wise to make one trip and to offer coffee to all of your customers. That way you are using your time wisely, anticipating your customers' needs, and providing good service.

Taking Advantage

Honesty and integrity are two qualities that will serve you well in the restaurant business.

Some servers attempt to please their customers by giving them extras with their meals and not charging for them. These extras could include dressings, condiments, bread, side dishes, and the like. Then, there are servers (who fortunately are in the minority) who treat their friends and family to drinks, desserts, and even whole meals without charging for them. The primary reason for this is that the server is hoping for a larger tip. The assumption is that the customer will leave as the tip what he would have paid for these extra items. However, this kind of conduct is not good for the business or for the server. Someone will find out: the customer will expect the same from another server and will complain either when he doesn't get the extra items or when he is charged for them. This will lead to an investigation, and if enough complaints lead back to the same server, that server will likely be disciplined or fired.

How to Handle Customer Complaints

Some customers complain at every opportunity, and some complain for no reason at all. Some customers complain because they got up on the wrong side of the bed. Some customers just want a discount or do not want to pay. Some customers compare service from one establishment to the next regardless of how much they have paid for their meals. Some customers are just unhappy. Then again, their complaints may have a legitimate reason. How do you handle a customer who complains?

a.   Listen very carefully while the customer talks.

b. Let the customer explain the reason for the complaint.

c. Don't argue, agree, or disagree with the customer.

d. If the customer's complaint is reasonable, use your judgment and do your best to make him happy. You do not want to lose him, regardless of whether he is a regular customer or a new customer.

For the establishment, reasonable concessions are a small price to pay, and the majority of customers will be satisfied and accept a compromise.

Accepting Customer Gifts

In order to show appreciation for special or ongoing good service at their favorite restaurant, many customers will bring gifts such as thank-you cards or Christmas cards, often containing money. Remember that customers are not obligated to do this, but if they see that a server has gone out of his way to accommodate them, they will often show their gratitude with some kind of token. You should always accept such gifts gracefully, with an appropriate thank you, acknowledging the customer's thoughtfulness.

9

Small Tips That Go a Long Way

Water: A Sign of Hospitality

Some restaurants make it a policy to serve water as soon as the customer sits down. Welcome all of your customers with a glass of water and a smile. Never wait for them to ask for it. Customers may need water for various reasons, such as to take prescription medication, vitamins, or simply because they would like water with their meal. It is also appropriate to offer refills when their glasses are empty.

Hot Tea

Providing a little extra hot water for the customer's tea before being asked is always a nice gesture. It prevents complaints and shows the customer that you are there to please her.

Iced Tea, Herbal Tea, and Flavored Teas

A server should always know what varieties of tea the restaurant offers and make the customer aware of the choices available. This can prevent many trips for the server or resentment on the part of a customer, who notices someone else has been offered a choice that they haven't.

Hot Water

How does a server treat the customer who asks for a cup of hot water? Some customers think a cup of hot water should be free. Sometimes they become quite angry when they are charged. It is very important to explain why they are being charged. Ask them to consider the hidden expenses, such as the dishwasher who will wash the cup, the soap consumed, the labor involved, the time of the server, and, in the case of an accident, the cost to replace the cup. Customers often do not see the underlying cost involved in what they think is just a cup of hot water.

Full Bar

A server should always ask the customer if he would like something from the bar either before or after the meal. The server can also recommend a nice glass of wine or a cocktail. Even if the customer has not thought about having a drink, he may change his mind once he hears the suggestion.

While the Customer Waits

If you work in a restaurant that offers newspapers, magazines, or tourist brochures to its customers, offer these items to your customers while they are waiting for their meals. They will keep them occupied and may be particularly helpful if they are new to the area. If they are tourists, they may also be able to plan their entertainment.

While the Customer Waits and Waits...

We have talked about busy shifts in restaurants and times when a server will have a lot on her plate (no pun intended). We have also talked about having a cooperative spirit and how helping out one's coworkers benefits all concerned. Now let's talk about how all of this may affect the customer.

Customers are usually forgiving when it comes to waiting a few extra minutes for their meal. However, no one wants to wait forty-five minutes for a meal that should take half the time to prepare. It is up to the server to try to make things right—and not by making excuses such as, "The kitchen is understaffed," "The restaurant is extremely busy," or "There is a backlog of orders." Whatever the reason, the server should always apologize for the delay and offer a complimentary drink, more coffee, or even a dessert on the house to make up for the lengthy inconvenience. (Always check with the management before you offer any free food or drinks so that you don't jeopardize your relationship with management.)

Never ignore a customer or avoid looking in her direction for fear of making eye contact and being put on the spot. You must go out of your way to smooth over any rough situation and keep the customer happy.

Just Desserts?

Always suggest dessert to the customer. Even if the customer has no intention of ordering dessert, he will appreciate being asked. Sometimes just asking will induce their desire to have dessert.

Doggy Bag

At the end of a customer's meal, the server should be aware of any customers who have not finished everything on their plate. There may be a number of reasons for this, especially with seniors. Customers may be full, there might have been too much food for one person, or they may prefer to have a portion of it later as a snack. In any case, it is appropriate for the server to offer a take-home container. Some customers may be too embarrassed to ask, especially if it is their first time in your restaurant or if it is an upscale establishment. When you ask, you are not only showing them that you are anticipating their wishes, but you are also preventing an uncomfortable situation for the shy customer.

Total Dining Experience

When most customers go out to dine, they are looking for the total dining experience. They want to enjoy a good meal, a comfortable atmosphere, and good service. Providing just two out of the three will not bring a customer back. Good service can be the icing on the cake!

10

Finishing Up

Presenting the Check

Always present the check to the customer by placing it on a clean section of the table—never set it beside dirty dishes or on a soiled section of the tablecloth. You should always accompany the check with a smile and a thank-you, or an expression such as, "Hope to see you again," or "Have a nice day."

Paying the Bill

If a customer pays the check with cash, don't assume that you can keep the change. Unless the customer has specifically told you to keep the change, always bring it back. There are occasions when the customer may intend to leave a tip greater than the amount of the change. For instance, imagine that a customer's bill is $36.50 and she gives you $40.00. You assume that she intended to leave you a $3.50 tip (not quite 10%) and decide that it's not what you deserve for the great service you gave. You assume that if you take the change back she may only leave you $2.00. You decide to keep the change and bluff your way through the situation. Not only will you offend the customer, but she may very well have intended to take away the change and replace it with a $5.00 bill, leaving a 15% gratuity. You may have cheated yourself and upset the customer with your little ploy.

This indiscretion happens all too often, in many different types of restaurants. It really highlights the ignorance of the server. In the end, you will come out ahead if give good service. Respect the fact that the tip a customer leaves is at his discretion.

Customers Who Pay with Credit Cards

Many customers choose to pay with credit cards. This is usually not a problem, but how does one handle a customer whose credit card has been declined? In those cases, take care to handle the situation with tact. You should never tell the customer his card has been declined in front of other guests. Sometimes the customer knows his credit card will be declined, but he takes a chance anyway. Avoid embarrassing the customer, give him the benefit of the doubt and ask, "Could I have another card, please?" If the customer becomes hostile, ask him to come with you, show him what the credit card machine has disclosed, and let the customer decide how he will pay. The customer should always leave satisfied.

Tips

Never express your opinions about tips in front of the customers. If you receive a poor tip, don't allow this to affect another person you are waiting on or the next customer at the table. Don't allow your attitude about one bad tip to cause a wave of bad tips. Even the best server will occasionally get customers who tip poorly or not at all. If there is a reason for the poor tip, try to correct the situation. If you honestly feel the service and food were good, and the customer even confirms this but still leaves very little, shrug it off and smile to yourself. Good servers know that they will encounter a wide range of people and tipping practices. They know that, generally, good service equals good tips. Not every table will leave a good tip, no matter how good the service and meal.

Another thing to keep in mind is never count your money in front of your customers. If you are leaving, don't go out on the floor to collect your tips after you have changed clothes. If you can't wait until the next time you come to work to get your money, ask someone who is still on duty to pick it up for you.

Credit Card Tips

Often, customers question the process used to distribute tips to the appropriate server. In these cases, it is up to the manager or cashier to explain how credit card tips are handled and to do so in a way that the customer will understand. Customers need to trust that their server will get the tip they left.

At the end of a shift, a server typically receives a credit card sales report with her own number or name. From the report, she can verify her total credit card sales and the credit card tips she should receive. Since each server knows her exact number of tables and customers served, she has the proof she needs to obtain the appropriate tips. Some establishments include the tip in the total cost of the bill on the report, but either way the server always gets the tip.

Conclusion

Perhaps the best advice in concluding this guide is also the simplest. Be yourself, be courteous, and be attentive to your customers. And always remember to smile!

978-0-595-35736-9
0-595-35736-9